Growing Things

Buds and Blossoms
A Book About Flowers

Written by Susan Blackaby
Illustrated by Charlene DeLage

Content Adviser: Jeffrey H. Gillman, Ph.D., Assistant Professor
Horticultural Science, University of Minnesota, St. Paul, Minnesota

Reading Adviser: Susan Kesselring, M.A., Literacy Educator
Rosemount-Apple Valley-Eagan (Minnesota) School District

PICTURE WINDOW BOOKS
Minneapolis, Minnesota

Editor: Nadia Higgins

Designer: Nathan Gassman

Page production: Picture Window Books

The illustrations in this book were painted with watercolor.

Picture Window Books

5115 Excelsior Boulevard

Suite 232

Minneapolis, MN 55416

1-877-845-8392

www.picturewindowbooks.com

Printed in the United States of America.

1 2 3 4 5 6 08 07 06 05 04 03

Library of Congress Cataloging-in-Publication Data

Blackaby, Susan.

Buds and blossoms : a book about flowers / written by Susan Blackaby ; illustrated by Charlene DeLage.

24 p. : #bill.   v. cm.   (Growing things)

Contents: Flower features—Shades and shapes—Insects, birds, and nectar—How pollen gets around

—How seeds begin to grow—Bugs and our planet—First class flowers—Fun facts.

ISBN 1-4048-0112-X (lib. bdg.)

1. Flowers—Juvenile literature. 2. Plants—Juvenile literature. [1. Flowers. 2. Plants.]

I. DeLage, Charlene, 1944- ill. II. Title.

QK49 .B525 2003

575.6—dc21

2002156329

Table of Contents

Flower Features

People like flowers because they are pretty,
but flowers are made to do a very special job.

Flowers hold all the plant parts that make new plants.

Shades and Shapes

Flowers come in a rainbow of colors.

Flowers smell sweet or fruity or spicy.

6

Flowers come in lots of graceful shapes.

Flower shapes tell how the petals form the flower.

Here are some common flower shapes:

Bell	Button	Cup
Drop	Globe	Spike
Star	Tube	Trumpet

Insects, Birds, and Nectar

Color, smell, and shape help flowers do their job.

Pretty flowers attract helpful insects, birds, and animals.

The insects, birds, and animals are on the hunt for nectar.
Nectar is the sweet, sticky juice inside of flowers.

Color makes flowers easy to spot if you are a hungry creature.

Some flowers even have markings that work like landing strips.
Streaks, stripes, or dots show creatures where to stop for food.

How Pollen Gets Around

Most flowers have male and female parts.

Yellow dust called pollen comes from the male part of the flower.

Without pollen, seeds cannot grow.

Creatures stick their beaks or noses or legs or bodies into the flower.
They sip the nectar. Grains of pollen stick to them.

Some flowers have special shapes.

Only one kind of creature can drink from each of these flowers.

Hummingbird
beaks fit down into
trumpet-shaped flowers.
Bumblebees can get inside
of tube-shaped flowers.

14

Creatures carry the grains of pollen to the next flower and the next. Grains of pollen get dropped along the way. Some pollen sticks to the female parts of flowers.

How Seeds Begin to Grow

When grains of pollen stick to the female
part of a flower, a pollen tube grows.
The pollen tube reaches an egg inside the flower.

The egg inside the flower is fertilized.

When the egg is fertilized, the seeds begin to grow.

Bugs and Our Planet

People need to be careful when they use bug sprays to get rid of pests.

Sprays can get rid of insects that carry pollen to flowers.

Sprays can get rid of insects that other helpful creatures eat.

What might happen to a plant without the creatures that pollinate flowers?

Go out into a garden. Smell a flower.
Bite into an apple. Climb a tree.

Think about the flowers and the creatures that help fill the world with plants, one grain of pollen at a time.

First-Class Flowers

Every state has a state flower.
Find out what your state flower is.
Use garden books to study pictures of your state flower.
Design a postage stamp with a picture of the state flower on it.
Use crayons, pens, colored pencils, or paint to create your finished stamp.

Fun Facts

- Some flowering plants are pollinated by bats.

- *Rafflesia arnoldii* is the largest flower in the world.
  It is 3 feet (1 meter) across.

- It can take a Giant Sequoia 175 to 200 years to produce flowers.

- A bee has to visit 2 million flowers to make one pound
  (one-half kilogram) of honey.

- A bee visits 50 to 100 flowers each time it leaves the hive.

- Broccoli is a flower that you can eat.

- There are more than 80 different kinds of sunflowers.

Words to Know

fertilize—to join male plant parts and female plant parts to make seeds

nectar—sweet liquid found in flowers. Nectar attracts hungry insects
and birds; bees use nectar to make honey.

pollen—fine, yellow dust made by flowers.
Pollen helps flowers make seeds.

pollinate—to carry pollen from the male part of the flower
to the female part

Flower Parts

The female part of the flower is called the pistil.
At the top of the pistil is the stigma.
The style connects the stigma to the ovary.
Inside the ovary are the egg cells.

The male part of a flower is called the stamen.
At the top of the stamen is the anther.
Pollen is the yellow dust on the tip of the anther.

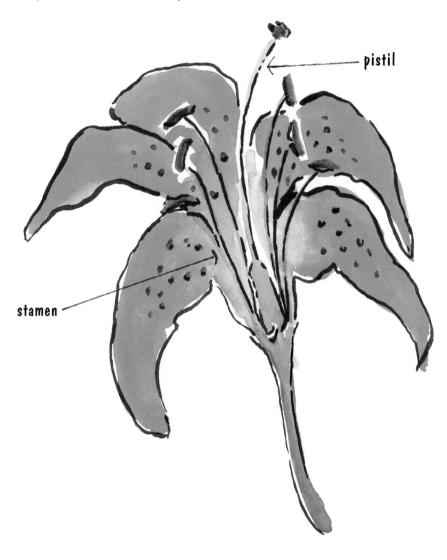

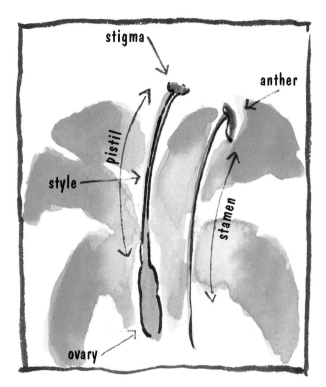

23

To Learn More

At the Library

Hammersmith, Craig. *Watch It Grow.* *Minneapolis:* Compass Point, 2002.

Royston, Angela. *How Plants Grow.* Des Plaines, Ill.: Heinemann Library, 1999.

Saunders-Smith, Gail. *From Bud to Blossom.* Mankato, Minn.: Pebble Books, 1998.

Spilsbury, Louise. *Plant Growth.* Chicago: Heinemann Library, 2002.

On the Web

California Native Plant Society Kids' Page
http://www.cnps.org/kidstuff/kidstuff.htm
For facts and activities on flowering plants

EPA Kids' Site
http://www.epa.gov/kids
For information about exploring and protecting nature

Want more information about flowers? FACT HOUND offers a safe, fun way to find Web sites. All of the sites on Fact Hound have been researched by our staff. Simply follow these steps:

1. Visit *http://www.facthound.com.*
2. Enter a search word or 140480112X.
3. Click Fetch It.

Your trusty Fact Hound will fetch the best sites for you!

Index